Famous Children's Authors

By
Shirley Norby and Gregory Ryan

The authors work as a librarian and second grade teacher at the Sea Girt Elementary School, Sea Girt, New Jersey where the library has achieved national recognition from the U.S. Department of Education for its "Library as a Classroom" Program.

Publishers
T.S. Denison & Co., Inc.
Minneapolis, Minnesota

DEDICATION

"For JoDee, who was touched by the joy of reading when she was very young, and for all those who bring children and books together."

Shirley Norby

"For Liz, Caitlin, and Abigail, of course! And for all my Second Graders, with heartfelt gratitude."

Gregory Ryan

Standard Book Number: 513-01907-3
Copyright ©1988 by T.S. Denison & Co., Inc.
Minneapolis, Minnesota 55431

Introduction for the Children

Babar, Curious George, the Cat in the Hat, and Ramona are some of the well-known story characters created by the authors and illustrators you will read about in this book. We selected these twenty people because they are popular with our students, their books are outstanding, and they are favorites of ours.

We work together in a small New Jersey elementary school near the Atlantic Ocean. As a teacher and a librarian, we have been bringing children and books together for over thirty-five years. We have shared story books, joke books, poetry books, books about monsters, athletes, and folk heroes. For a long time we looked for a book about authors and illustrators, but we could not find one that was just right for our students. So we decided to write one.

We started by reading library books and magazine articles about these men and women. We also wrote letters to them asking questions about their childhood experiences, families, school memories, pets - things that were not found in the library. Many of them wrote back to us with their answers. We put all that information together and wrote it down to share with you. We had great fun writing this book and we hope you and your friends will have fun reading it. Each author story is followed by a list of their book titles, so you will know what to ask for when you go to the library. Some of the books you will be able to enjoy now. Others you may have to read when you are a little older.

As you read this book, you will be interested to find that many of these writers decided when they were very young that they would like to create stories or pictures when they were all grown-up. Have you ever thought that perhaps *you* would like to be an author or illustrator when you grow up? The best way to prepare is to start right now by reading, reading, reading! Also, you can get started by writing stories on your own. Share them with your teacher and family. Illustrate your stories or ask a friend to illustrate them for you. Make a book of your own stories and give it as a gift to someone special. As soon as you finish one project, get started on another one.

Perhaps one day you will write or illustrate a book which millions of people will enjoy and they will read all about **you** in a book of *FAMOUS CHILDREN'S AUTHORS.*

A Message to Teachers and Librarians

• After you have shared a biographical sketch with your class, make a collection of that author's books available on your classroom reading shelf. Your children will become enthused about being among the first in the class to read the books written by the author you have just introduced. Reading partners can share the books and plan projects together.

• Keep an eye out for new books by these authors as they become available. Your students will scramble to be the first to read these hot-off-the-press books as they arrive at your school.

• Encourage your young readers to design posters advertising new and old book friends. Decorate your walls and halls with these colorful attention getters. Build excitement with a sign-up "Reservation List" for the books they just can't wait to read.

• Help small committees to prepare short weekly promotional "Author Spotlights" to broadcast over your school's loud speaker system. Groups of Individual students can design and construct original book jackets to add a personal touch to these author wall displays.

• While professional authors are very busy people, many of them would welcome a class fan letter giving the children's reactions to their work.

• Using index cards, children construct a Book Character 'matching' game. One card gives the character's name. Shuffle the cards and lay them out on the table. Playing alone or with a friend, the child matches the character description card and the name card.

• Construct an 'Author - Book Title' matching game, as above.

• Older children can construct a computer database using author biographical and bibliographical information for various fields in the data base.

• Students keep journals as if they were a character in a favorite book. Do this for one week (or two) and change to another character.

• Write an original story based on a familiar book character. (e.g. *Curious George Goes to the Olympics.*)

• Create a comic strip that simply summarizes a favorite book. Use new vocabulary words from the book.

• Tape record a book you have shared, so the children can enjoy it again and again at home or at school.

• On index cards, children design and write picture postcards that their favorite book characters might send home to their authors.

• Children design bookmarks to advertise their favorite books. Make them available at your library's circulation desk.

• Invent a new ending for a favorite story.

• Create sock puppets for your favorite book characters. Put on a puppet show for the kindergarteners.

• Create a bulletin board display for a favorite author. Have it in his/her birthday month. Celebrate with a birthday reading party.

• Two children research a favorite author together. One of them acts as an interviewer asking pertinent questions of the 'author' student. Perform the interview for the class as a talk-show segment. Videotape these to show to other classes.

• Create a time-line using author biographical and bibliographical information. This can be done separately for individual authors or collectively as year-long class project.

• These suggestions are just the beginning. We hope *FAMOUS CHILDREN'S AUTHORS* will spark many more creative ideas to enliven your class or library.

Table of Contents

Harry Allard

It is not considered polite to call people stupid, but Harry Allard has created a whole family of "stupids" in his stories for children. In the Allard books the Stupid family is never embarrassed by their mistakes because they do not realize they are being ridiculous. Readers can laugh at Mr. and Mrs. Stupid, the two Stupid kids, their dog named Kitty, and an assortment of Stupid relatives in three different books: *The Stupids Step Out, The Stupids Have A Ball,* and *The Stupids Die.* Of course, the Stupids don't really die. They just think they are dead for awhile when all the lights go out in their house one night.

In another series of books the author has gone back to school and created a classroom (Room 207), the nicest teacher in the school (Miss Nelson), and her dreaded substitute (Viola Swamp). Are the Swamp and Miss Nelson the same person? Readers have to figure this out for themselves because the class in Room 207 never knows for sure. *Miss Nelson Is Missing, Miss Nelson Is Back,* and *Miss Nelson Has A Field Day* are all about school, teachers, the principal, and children who are sometimes naughty and sometimes good. Whether or not you like your teacher, you will enjoy reading about Miss Nelson and the children in Room 207.

Harry Allard didn't like school when he was a child, but he went anyway for many more years than was required. He is now a college teacher of French in Massachusetts. He can be called Dr. Allard because he has a "Doctor of Philosophy" (Ph.D.) degree from Yale University. He lived and worked in Paris, France for three years and can speak French fluently. He can also read Spanish and German, and is able to translate Latin and Greek. He likes to listen to classical music and cook Hindu food. His pets are an eleven year old, blind, French bulldog named Olga, and two alley cats named Phyllis and Charlestown.

When Harry Allard was a child, his family was very poor. He was born in Evanston, Illinois in 1928. He didn't read children's books much as a child, but he loved archaeology and remembers a book called Buried Cities by Jennie Hall as being a favorite of his in the fourth grade. He hated sports in school and says that he still does.

Harry Allard met James Marshall, the author and illustrator of the *"George and Martha"* books while they were both living in Charlestown, Massachusetts. They became friends and have worked together on all the *"Stupids"* and *"Miss Nelson"* books. James Marshall does the drawings and Harry Allard writes the stories. When people work together on books like this it is called a collaboration. Allard and Marshall have collaborated on several award winning books. They also work alone and have published books they have worked on by themselves. Harry Allard's own favorite book is not one of the *"Stupids"* or *"Miss Nelson"* titles, but is called, *It's So Nice to Have a Wolf Around the House.* Look for it in the library or on television because it was made into a full-length cartoon feature. He says that he is the old man in the book and that it is a story about himself.

Readers can say, as the Stupids so often do, "It certainly has been fun!" Thank you, Mr. Allard for writing 'stupendous' books that make us laugh!

A Selection of Books by
Harry Allard
It's So Nice To Have A Wolf Around The House
The Stupids Step Out
The Stupids Have A Ball
The Stupids Die
Miss Nelson Is Missing
Miss Nelson Is Back
Miss Nelson Has A Field Day
There's A Party At Mona's Tonight
I Will Not Go To Market Today
Bumps In The Night
The Tutti-Frutti Case

Stan and Jan Berenstain

As a child, Jan Grant's favorite books were ones with wonderful pictures. She loved A *Children's Garden of Verses, The World Book of Nursery Rhymes,* and *Alice's Adventures in Wonderland.* Her father was a carpenter and an artist, so she always had pencils and paper around when she felt like drawing her favorite storybook characters. She also loved to copy pictures from the Sunday comics.

Stan Berenstain enjoyed looking at art books as a child and he soon tried out his own artistic talents. He remembers that his "first masterpiece — a huge boxing mural painted right on the dining room wall — was not appreciated" so he started painting on pieces of cardboard that came from the laundry in his father's shirts. Like Jan, he enjoyed drawing characters from the newspaper comics.

Stan and Jan grew up in Philadelphia and met for the first time when they were students at the Philadelphia College of Art in the 1940's. When World War II started, Stan joined the Army and became an artist drawing medical pictures to help the Army doctors. Jan did not join the Army, but she got a job drawing and making airplanes. While Stan was in the Army he started selling cartoons to magazines to earn extra money.

After the war, Stan returned to art school and soon married Jan, who already had a job as an art teacher. The new Mr. and Mrs. Berenstain teamed up to create magazine cartoons together, including the very popular *It's All in the Family* which first appeared in 1953. To this day, all their work: cartoons, children's books, and even television specials, are done as a team!

Their most famous creations, of course, are the "bumptious bear family" books which they began publishing in 1962, *The Berenstain Bears.* They started doing these books when their own two sons, Leo and Michael were young. The boys loved Dr. Seuss because his stories made them laugh out loud. So Stan and Jan began writing picture books about funny things that happen to families.

Many of their Bear books are about ordinary things; going out for a team, going to camp or the doctor or dentist for the first time, or moving to a new home. One story, Mama's *New Job,* tells how the Bears get along when Mama Bear opens a store to sell the beautiful quilts that she designs and makes. Brother Bear, Sister Bear, and Papa Bear find out that Mama can manage a store and still be a terrific mother and wife. In fact, when everyone pitches in around the house, everyone is a lot happier.

People often ask Stan and Jan why they use Bears for their stories. They explain that bear stories have always been popular with children. Everyone loves *Goldilocks and the Three Bears.* And bears can stand up. So their funny, furry Bears are all dressed up just like people, but without shoes.

Since their Bear Family books are read by millions of children in over thirteen countries, it seems that people do like to read funny family books.

Maybe this Mom and Pop artist team ought to be called Stan and Jan BEARenstain.

A Selection of Books by
Stan and Jan Berenstain

The Berenstain Bears' Trouble at School

The Berenstain Bears Go Out for the Team

The Berenstain Bears and the Trouble with Friends

The Berenstain Bears Get Stage Fright

The Berenstain Bears and the Week at Grandma's

The Berenstain Bears and Too Much Birthday

The Berenstain Bears Forget Their Manners

The Berenstain Bears Learn About Strangers

The Berenstain Bears and Mama's New Job

The Berenstain Bears and Too Much T.V.

The Berenstain Bears and the Messy Room

The Berenstain Bears and the Truth

The Berenstain Bears ' Trouble with Money

The Berenstain Bears Get in a Fight

The Berenstain Bears Go to Camp

The Berenstain Bears and the Sitter

The Berenstain Bears' Moving Day

The Berenstain Bears Visit the Dentist

The Berenstain Bears' Science Fair

The Berenstain Bears' Almanac

The Berenstain Bears and the Big Road Race

Reprinted with permission of Stan & Jan Berenstain.
Front cover illustration for *The Berenstain Bears and Mama's New Job.*
Written and illustrated by Stan & Jan Berenstain.
Copyright ©1984 by Berenstains, Inc.
Published by Random House, Inc., N.Y.

Judy Blume

Judy Sussman Blume was born in Elizabeth, New Jersey. She is the daughter of Dr. Rudolph and Esther Sussman. When she was a little girl, Judy was a great pretender. She loved playing detective with her friends, making up and solving mysteries. She also took ballet and piano lessons. She often put on her own shows and dreamed that someday she would be famous. Today she is still a pretender, but she pretends on paper now. She may not be a ballerina or a pianist, but she is one of the world's most famous writers.

Judy Blume says that one thing that helps her to write the way she does is that she has an excellent memory. She can remember just about everything that ever happened to her as far back as the third grade, and many things from even before that. For instance, Judy remembers how embarrassed she was in kindergarten one day when she cried in front of the whole class because another child had stepped on her finger.

When she was in third grade, her older brother David became ill and to help him recover, her parents decided it would be good for him to spend the winter in a place where it was warm. So Judy and David went to Florida for the winter with their mother and grandmother. Many years later, Judy wrote about this adventure in her book, *Sally J. Freedman As Herself.*

Judy's favorite book as a child was *Madeline* by Ludwig Bemelmans. She loved the book so much that she took it out of the library and hid it in the toy drawer in her kitchen so she could keep it forever. She thought that it was the only copy of the book in the world and she didn't want to give it up. She read it so many times that she could recite it by heart. She can still recite it to this very day.

All during her childhood Judy made up imaginary stories in her head, but she became a "real" writer while she was in Battin High School. In her junior year she became a reporter for the school newspaper and in her senior year she became the feature editor.

Judy Blume had planned to become a second grade teacher. In her second year at college she met and fell in love with a young lawyer, John Blume. Even before she finished college she married John. Soon after graduating, her daughter Randy was born and two years later, her son Larry was born. Her teaching career never did get started.

When Randy and Larry were old enough to go to nursery school, Judy wanted to do something outside the home. Since her interest was in writing, she signed up for a night class in writing. She really enjoyed the weekly homework assignments. Her teacher was so helpful and encouraging that Judy signed up for the course a second time. Judy Blume did not become a famous writer overnight. She sent lots of stories to publishers and was very upset and disappointed when they told her that her stories were not good enough to be published. She kept trying and eventually in 1969, *The One in the Middle is the Green Kangaroo* was published. Since then Judy Blume has written over seventeen books.

People are often surprised to find out that Judy Blume has written books not just for young children, but also for teenagers and adults. She hopes that adults who read her grown-up stories will go back and read what she has written for children, and children will read her grown-up stories when they get older then they will really know who Judy Blume is and what she is like.

When Judy was a young teenager she often went to summer camp where she learned to swim. You can read all about her experiences at camp in *Otherwise Known As Sheila the Great.* When she was fifteen, she received a phone call at camp from her mother telling her the shocking news that her grandmother had died. This memory helped her to write *Forever.* Another one of her books, *It's Not the End of the World,* shows how one family gets through the pain of a divorce without the whole world coming to an end.

Death, divorce, moving, and growing up are the kinds of problems that are found in Judy Blume's books. One reason she writes these kinds of books is because she thinks that kids live in the same world as adults and that they see and hear things that sometimes upset them. Family problems or other worries only get worse when they are kept secret. The best thing to do is to talk the problems over with someone you love and trust. But if you do not have anyone to talk things over with, you can at least read about the problem in a book and know that other people have gone through the same thing.

One of Judy Blume's best-loved characters is Farley Dexter Hatcher, or "Fudge" as he is better known. *Tales of a Fourth Grade Nothing* introduces us to this nutty two-year old who drives his big brother crazy. Judy Blume based this book partly on a newspaper story about a little boy who really did swallow a pet turtle, and partly on the antics of her own son Larry. Fudge became so popular that she wrote another story about him called, *Superfudge.* The story is not only great fun, but it also has some good ideas about what it is like for a family to move to a new neighborhood, for parents to change jobs, and for children to go to a new school and make new friends.

The story for one of her latest books, *Just As Long As We're Together,* rolled around in her head for several years before she put it down on paper. Writing the first draft of a new story is the hardest part for Judy. Her favorite part is rewriting it. She rewrites a story five or six times before she gets it just right for publication. But then she feels sad, because sending the book off to the publisher is like saying good-bye to an old friend.

Each old friend that Judy Blume says good-bye to is greeted as a new friend by the millions of readers who enjoy her books.

A Selection of Books by
Judy Blume

Tales of a Fourth Grade Nothing
Superfudge
Starring Sally J. Freedman As Herself
Blubber
It's Not the End of the World
Then Again, Maybe I Won't
Iggie's House
Deenie
Are You There, God? It's Me, Margaret.
Otherwise Known As Sheila the Great
Just as Long as We're Together

Mary Calhoun

"I decided at the age of seven to be an author,
and I've stuck to the idea, more or less, ever since."

Born on August 3, 1926 in Keokuk, Iowa, Mary Louise Huiscamp grew up in an old brick house built by her great-grandfather just two blocks away from where the mighty Mississippi River snakes along between Iowa and Illinois. The great, old house, built in 1871, was too large for one family to fill, so Mary's mother took in renters who paid money to live there. Some of the renters were quite unusual. One of them claimed to be a gypsy. Another was a high wire walker for the Street Fair. And one group of men and women turned out to be wanted by the police.

As a child, Mary's mother told her stories. Lots of stories! Her favorite ones were about fairies and brownies. *(Even today, when she herself is a grandmother, Mary still hopes to meet a real brownie!)* Mary was so interested in her mother's stories that she started learning how to read, with her mother's help, when she was only four years old.

"By the time I was seven I was a full-fledged reader and choosing books from the public library which was only two-and-a-half blocks away. The *Old Mother West Wind* books were my earliest favorites, closely followed by *The Adventures of a Brownie*," she recalls.

As with all "river kids," the Mississippi River played a large part in her childhood. Her book *Making the Mississippi Shout* is about a boy who wanted to make the river "shout with music" by playing the calliope on a paddle boat. Many of her other childhood memories have found their way into her *Katie John* books. Mark Twain is one of her favorite writers, and when you are older and read his stories, you will see why.

As a teenager Mary worked full-time each summer at the public library and gave story hours for the children. To this day, one of her favorite pastimes is story telling, and she is often invited to schools and sometimes to libraries to share folktales, or tall tales, or stories she has made up. Many of the stories are retold in her books.

When she went to college she studied newspaper writing and worked part-time for different newspapers. In 1948, she graduated with a degree in journalism. Ms. Calhoun says that newspaper work taught her to write without wasting words. It taught her to choose just the right word to create just the right picture in the reader's mind.

Mary is the mother of two sons, Michael and Gregory. As a young mother she often dropped her household chores to tell stories to Mike and Greg. The boys enjoyed these stories so much that Mary started writing them down. Soon after this, her first two books were published.

Today, Mary admits that she gets ideas for her stories at all different times and in all different places; while ironing, knitting, or even in the bathtub! While she has written books for many age groups, the picture book is her favorite type of writing. "There's a special delight in forming the picture book story, where every word, every thought, counts!" This was an important lesson she had learned during her days working at the newspaper.

Her two boys are grown now and she has four grandchildren. She lives in Steamboat Springs, Colorado with her husband. Their home is in the Rocky Mountains, near Routt National Forest. Her love for nature and wildlife show up in her books *Cross Country Cat* and *Audubon Cat.* She also enjoys swimming, skiing, hiking, and bird watching.

Other books of hers like *The Runaway Brownie, Mermaid of Storms,* and *Mrs. Dog's Own House* may have started out as stories that she tells at the libraries that she still visits. The Rangely Public Library in Colorado liked her work so much, that the children's wing of the library was named in her honor.

A sonnet is a very difficult type of poem to write and Mary Calhoun finds writing a good picture book to be just as difficult. When talking about her writing, Mary once said, "I try to put as much thought and effort into each of my stories as William

Shakespeare must have put into one little sonnet."

When you read any of Mary Calhoun's forty-four books, you will agree that all of her hard work is well worth it.

A Selection of Books by Mary Calhoun

Big Sixteen
The Night the Monster Came
Hot-Air Henry
Audubon Cat
Cross-Country Cat
The Battle of Reubin Robin and Kite Uncle John
The Hungry Leprechaun
Jack the Wise and the Cornish Cuckoos
The Witch of Hissing Hill
The Witch's Pig: A Cornish Folktale
Wobble, The Witch Cat
Katie John
Depend on Katie John
Honestly, Katie John!
Katie John and Heathcliff

It's Getting Beautiful Now
Ownself
White Witch of Kynance
The Witch Who Lost Her Shadow
The Horse Comes First
Camels Are Meaner Than Mules
The House of Thirty Cats
Making the Mississippi Shout
Nine Lives of Homer C. Cat
Mermaid of Storms
The Runaway Brownie
River-Minded Boy
Magic in the Alley
Traveling Ball of String

Reprinted with permission
Cross Country Cat, written by Mary Calhoun, Illustrated by E. Ingraham.
Copyright ©1979.
Illustration of Henry.

Eric Carle

Eric Carle Remembers:

"*Friendship is so important among the very young. I still remember my first friendship which lasted from years one to six. Then I had to move from my home in Syracuse, New York to Germany with my parents and I not only moved away from my best friend but I left a school that I loved. When I got to Germany I had to learn two languages and how to get along in a country that was far different from the one I was used to. Often I wished that a bridge could be built from Germany to America so I could get back home. My German school was very strict and I hated it most of the time. When World War II broke out my father had to go into the German Army. He was away for eight years and was a prisoner of war in Russia part of the time. I missed my father very much.*"

After the war Eric Carle studied art in Germany and began working there as a poster designer. In 1950 he returned to the United States to live and found many different kinds of jobs to do. He designed book jackets and advertising material and began illustrating books for children. The first books he illustrated were beginning readers, just like the books often used in first grade classrooms. Eric Carle found that he really liked illustrating books for children and he began to make books for himself, becoming an author and illustrator.

The first book he did alone was called *1,2,3, to the Zoo*. It won first prize for picture books at a book fair in Italy and the Children's Book Prize in Germany in 1970. *The Very Hungry Caterpillar, The Secret Birthday Message,* and *Have You Seen My Cat?* are some of his other books that have won awards and are fun to read. Often they are full of surprises; pages with holes or uneven edges or they have an ending that makes you want to read the book over again, but backwards this time!

Eric Carle often uses a technique called collage to illustrate his books. Collage is making a picture by pasting paper, cloth, or other things to a flat surface. Eric Carle uses multi-colored tissue paper, paint, crayons and rubber cement to create his collages. He has a special room in his home called a studio where he can do his art work and write everyday.

Charlemont, Massachusetts is where Eric Carle lives now with his wife, two cats and a dog. He has two grown-up children, Rolf and Cirsten. His son is a painter and his daughter is a graphic designer and photographer. Mrs. Carle works with handicapped children.

When asked which of his books he likes best he says, *"Do You Want To Be My Friend?* is my favorite because it is about friendship among children."* Eric Carle has made many friends among children who read and love his books.

A Selection of Books by
Eric Carle

All About Arthur (an absolutely absurd ape)
Do You Want To Be My Friend?
Have You Seen My Cat?
I See a Song
Pancakes, Pancakes!
Seven Stories by Hans Christian Andersen
The Rooster Who Set Out to See the World
The Secret Birthday Message
The Very Hungry Caterpillar
The Grouchy Ladybug
1,2,3 to the Zoo
The Mixed Up Chameleon
What's for Lunch
Eric Carle's Storybook: Seven Tales by the Brothers Grimm
The Very Busy Spider
Let's Paint a Rainbow
The Honeybee and the Robber
12 Tales from Aesop
Catch the Ball

Beverly Cleary

Beezus, Ramona, Henry Huggins, Ribsy, and Ralph S. Mouse are familiar names to readers of Beverly Cleary's books and soon they will appear on television. Because of their popularity as books, *Ralph S. Mouse, The Mouse and the Motorcycle,* and *Runaway Ralph* are being adapted for television as is *Ramona the Pest.* Ramona is going to be made into a ten part series which should be ready for viewing in November or December of 1988.

How does Beverly Cleary get her good ideas for the characters in her stories? She says that she gets them, "From my own experience and from the world around me." She grew up as an only child on a farm in Oregon and lived there enjoying the freedom of farm life, until her family moved to the large city of Portland, Oregon when she was only six. There she began school. Life in a big city, sickness, being part of a large first grade class with a teacher who did not like her, and finding herself in the lowest reading group made her feel frightened and humiliated. Her first year of school was unhappy, but in the second grade she had a wonderful teacher, and she learned to like reading and writing. She wrote many letters to relatives and friends when she was a child. Today she recommends that children write letters too. *Dear Mr. Henshaw* is a Cleary book about a boy writing letters to someone he admires and how this makes his life less lonely.

Beverly Cleary's mother was helpful in getting her to read when she was in the primary grades. Her mother would borrow many books from the Oregon State Library and read them aloud to Beverly. Her mother read to her until she was in the fifth or sixth grade because there was no television then for entertainment. Beverly Cleary still loves to read and her favorite books now are English novels and biographies. She also likes to sew and travel when she has the time.

When Beverly Cleary finished elementary school and high school she went to college and studied to become a children's librarian. She worked as a librarian and also worked in a book store during the Christmas season. She always intended to write for children and one day she sat down at her typewriter and started *Henry*

Huggins, her first book. She was already married with twin children, Marianne and Malcolm, and it wasn't easy to write in her home with the sounds of children and the neighborhood all around her. However, some of the sounds from the outdoors have appeared in her books. *Ramona* is one of these 'accidents'. One day a neighbor calling for a little sister shouted, "Ra-mo-na!" and Beverly Cleary decided to name the character she was working on Ramona. The rest is history because Ramona has appeared in many Beverly Cleary books and is probably her favorite character. When asked why Ramona is her favorite, the author replies, "She is just a little girl overcoming obstacles and I like her." Beverly Cleary won't tell if the Quimby family will change in future books, but she thinks there may be more stories published about Ramona.

Beverly Cleary thinks about a book for about three years before beginning it, and then spends between six months to a year doing the actual writing. She writes in a small space at the end of a room in her California home. Her twins are grown up now so there is more quiet time in the house, but she is busier now than ever. She receives many letters from her readers which keep her in touch with children like you. She tries to personally answer most of her mail, but sometimes when she is very busy her publishing company will answer her letters for her.

Beverly Cleary's books appear in over ten countries and in a variety of languages. Many of her books have won important book awards including the Newbery Medal in 1984 for *Dear Mr. Henshaw.* This award is given each year to the most distinguished American book for children. Two of her *Ramona* books won the Newbery runner-up awards called Honor Books. You can find her Newbery Award books by looking for the gold or silver medals on the book covers. Beverly Cleary is one of America's best loved authors for children.

A Selection of Books by
Beverly Cleary

(Ages 3-6)
Janet's Thingamajigs
The Real Hole
Two Dog Biscuits
(Ages 4-8)
Lucky Chuck
(Ages 8-12)
Beezus and Ramona
Dear Mr. Henshaw (1984 Newbery Medal)
Ellen Tebbits
Emily's Runaway Imagination
Henry and Beezus
Henry and the Clubhouse
Henry and the Paper Route
Henry and Ribsy
Henry Huggins
Mitch and Amy
The Mouse and the Motorcycle
Otis Spofford
Ralph S. Mouse
Ramona and Her Father (a 1978 Newbery Honor Book)
Ramona and Her Mother
Ramona Forever
Ramona Quimby, Age 8 (a 1982 Newbery Honor Book)
Ramona the Brave
Ramona the Pest
Ribsy
Runaway Ralph
Socks
(Ages 12 up)
Fifteen
Jean and Johnny
The Luckiest Girl
Sister of the Bride
(Diaries to read and write in - Ages 8-12)
The Beezus and Ramona Diary
The Ramona Quimby Diary

Laurent de Brunhoff

**Bedtime is the time for
fantastic stories.**

One warm night in a quiet country house near Paris, France, when Laurent de Brunhoff was only five years old, his mother Cecile invented a bedtime story for him and his little brother. It was all about a baby elephant living in a forest. The boys enjoyed the story so much that they told their father, Jean de Brunhoff all about it. Jean (whose name in English would be "John") was an excellent artist and soon began painting the scenes and characters from the bedtime story. He gave the elephant a name and put everything together to make the first *Story of Babar,* which was published in France in 1931. Children and grown-ups immediately fell in love with this elephant, who is dressed in a bright green suit. With his pencils and watercolors, Jean created six more jumbo-sized Babar books before he died of a lung disease in 1937. But thanks to Jean's talented son, Laurent, the world has enjoyed over thirty more *Babar* books.

Laurent, the elder son of his painter/father and musician/mother, also enjoyed painting. When he was just twelve years old he was asked to help his uncle put the finishing touches on the paintings for a Babar book his father had started but left unfinished: *Babar Meets Father Christmas.* For the next few years he continued to paint on his own, but it wasn't until after World War II, when he was twenty-one years old that he created his first original Babar book: *Babar and That Rascal Arthur,* which was published in 1945. Since he had grown up with stories of Babar, he felt that King Babar and Queen Celeste were real members of his family, and so it was easy for him to pick up the adventures where his father Jean had left off. This book was so good that people did not notice at first that it was not written by Jean de Brunhoff. They thought it had just been the War that made them wait so long for a new Babar book. They did not realize that Babar had a new creator, the young Laurent de Brunhoff.

Laurent and his wife Marie-Claude have two children of their own, Ann and Antoine. Many of Laurent's ideas for new Babar books, such as *Babar and the*

Professor, come from his family life. The de Brunhoff's live in an apartment in Paris, but they also have a beach house on an island out in the Atlantic Ocean. This may have given him some ideas for the book *Babar at the Seashore. Babar's Mystery* has a lighthouse in it that is based on a real lighthouse near their beach home.

When Laurent is not creating books, he likes to garden and go birdwatching. See what Babar books you can find that have Laurent's hobbies in them.

Laurent says that he has no trouble thinking up new Babar books because ideas are always popping into his head. *"Babar appears at the tip of my pencil as if I had invented him myself."* Though he has written some books without elephants in them he says, *"My main activity is Babar and I still have such fun with him."*

Monsieur de Brunhoff's artwork sometimes travels to art galleries in different parts of the United States. Watch for an exhibition near you and go with your family to visit King Babar and Queen Celeste "in person."

The stories of Babar, Celeste, Pom, Flora, Alexander, and Isabelle are enjoyed in seventeen languages including German, Spanish, Danish, Hungarian, Hebrew, Japanese, and English. After creating all of these wonderful Babar books for children, parents, and grandparents to enjoy, all we can say is "Bravo, Laurent! Merci!" "Well done! Thank You!"

A Selection of Books by
Laurent de Brunhoff

Serafina the Giraffe
Captain Serafina
Anatole and His Donkey
Bonhomme
Bonhomme and the Huge Monster
Babar's Cousin: That Rascal Arthur
Babar's Picnic
Babar's Visit to the Bird Island
Babar's Fair Will Be Opened Next Sunday
Babar and the Professor
Babar's Castle
Babar Comes to America
Babar Loses His Crown
Babar Saves the Day

Babar Goes Skiing
Babar the Gardener
Babar Goes on a Picnic
Babar at the Seashore
Babar and the Doctor
Babar Learns to Drive
Babar Goes Visiting
Babar's Moon Trip
Babar's Birthday Surprise
Babar Keeps Fit
Babar the Artist
Babar the Camper
Babar Visits Another Planet
Babar and the Wully-Wully
Gregory and the Lady Turtle in the Valley of the
Magic Trees

Tomie dePaola

Tomie dePaola (pronounced "de-POW-la") laughs gleefully while reading a letter from one of his young readers.

"Dear Mr. dePaola,
Thank you for writing The Quicksand Book. I liked it very much. I especially like the directions you gave for how to make quicksand. This could be the perfect way to get rid of my pesty sister! Thanks again.
Your New Friend,"

Letters like this one make Mr. dePaola laugh right out loud. Laughter comes easily to this happy man and to the millions of readers who enjoy his books.

Tomie dePaola always wanted to be an artist and began to paint when he was only four years old. He also loved listening to stories and remembers his mother reading aloud to him every night when he was small. Folktales, legends, and a book called *Hitty, Her First Hundred Years* by Rachel Field were among his childhood favorites.

He remembers drawing all through his school years and after graduating from high school, he attended a special art college, The Pratt Institute. He studied there for four years and learned to work with different kinds of paints, papers, brushes, pens, and other materials that artists use.

Following graduation from college he started working as an illustrator and after many years of showing his drawings to publishers he was finally given a book to illustrate, a book called *Sound.* This was a dream come true! Since then he has drawn the pictures for over 100 books. Some of them have been written by other people, but most of them have Tomie dePaola's name on the cover as author and illustrator.

Strega Nona, Big Anthony, Nana Upstairs and Nana Downstairs, St. Francis, Mary and her Lamb, and Helga are just some of the characters who parade through the villages, streets, forests, fields, and houses in dePaola's colorful stories. His sketch of a heart, a bird, or one of his cats appear frequently on the pages of his books and serve as the artist's autograph to his readers.

Tomie dePaola lives in a red New England farmhouse in New Hampshire. He has a studio in his home and, when he is not traveling, he works there everyday. He has never married, but Bingley (an Airedale dog), Satie, Rosalie, and Conrad (his Abyssinian cats), all share his life and his home.

So many people write to him that he has a secretary to help with answering mail and who also takes care of his pets while Tomie is traveling around doing research, or giving speeches, or appearing on television. Often he is invited to appear in book stores where he autographs his books and talks to the children who have come to meet him. Children who know that popcorn is his favorite food often bring him bags of popcorn to these autographing parties. Even though popcorn fights are not allowed, meeting Tomie dePaola is always a fun-filled treat for people of all ages.

The villagers in his *Strega Nona* and *Big Anthony* books often say thank you to Strega Nona by using the Italian word "grazia." We can echo those words by saying "Grazia, Tomie dePaola! Grazia!" for giving us so many wonderful books! We look forward to your next one. And your next one. And your next one.

A Selection of Books by
Tomie dePaola

Andy: That's My Name
Big Anthony and the Magic Ring
Bill and Pete
"Charlie Needs a Cloak"
The Christmas Pageant
The Cloud Book
The Clown of God
David and Goliath
The Family Christmas Tree Book
Fin M'Coul, the Giant of Knockmany Hill
Flicks
Francis, the Poor Man of Assisi
The Friendly Beasts
Helga's Downoery, A Troll Love Story
The Hunter and the Animals
The Kids' Cat Book
The Knight and the Dragon
The Lady of Guadalupe

The Legend of the Bluebonnet
Marianna May and Nursey
Michael Bird-Boy
The Mysterious Giant of Barletta
Nana Upstairs and Nana Downstairs
Noah and the Ark
Now One Foot, Now the Other
Oliver Button is a Sissy
Pancakes for Breakfast
The Popcorn Book
The Prince of the Dolomites
The Quicksand Book
Sing, Pierrot, Sing
The Story of the Three Wise Kings
Strega Nona
Strega Nona's Magic Lessons
Tomie dePaola's Mother Goose
Watch Out for the Chicken Feet in Your Soup
The Comic Adventures of Old Mother Hubbard and Her Dog

Reprinted with permission of Holiday House.
Illustration from *The Popcorn Book*, by Tomie dePaola.
Copyright ©1978. Published by Holiday House.

Paul Galdone

Paul Galdone was born in Hungary and moved to the United States when he was fourteen. His family first settled in New Jersey where Paul attended high school. He did not speak English so he had to attend three English classes every day in order to learn the language quickly. Later his family decided to move to New York City where Paul was needed to help earn money for the family. He worked at different jobs during the day and attended art school at night. When he finished art school he found a job in the art department of a book publishing company and there he had the chance to design his first book jacket. He found that he loved everything about book illustrating and became so well thought of as a designer of book jackets that he left the publishing house for a career as a free-lance designer. As a free-lancer he worked for many different publishers in his own art studio at home. During his lifetime he illustrated children's books for twenty-five different publishers.

Paul Galdone always loved the outdoors and after spending four years in the Army, he moved from New York City to Rockland County in New York state. There he could walk in a nearby woods, plant a garden, and have room for assorted pets. He married and had two children; a daughter, Joanna, and a son, Paul Ferencz. Eventually, the family bought a farm in Tunbridge, Vermont where they spent summer vacations hiking and sketching.

Paul Galdone illustrated two Caldecott Honor books: *Anatole* and *Anatole and the Cat*. Both were written by Eve Titus. After spending many years illustrating other people's books he decided to do his own picture books. He chose to retell favorite classic tales such as H*enny Penny, The Horse, The Fox, and the Lion, The Three Bears, The Three Little Pigs, The Three Blind Mice,* plus many others. He also did a book with his daughter, Joanna, called *The Tailypo*. This is a popular ghost story that Joanna first heard her grandfather tell. Joanna Galdone is a teacher and she knew that children would love the story of *Tailypo*. She researched different versions of the story and wrote the one that appears in the book with illustrations by her father.

The Frog Prince was Paul Galdone's favorite Brothers Grimm fairy tale. He adapted and illustrated this tale in a book that was published in 1975. He used real frogs for models of the frog prince. He would catch frogs in the pond on his Vermont farm and quickly sketch their movements before returning them to the water. The frogs didn't seem to mind posing for the pages of the fairy tale. In fact, they seem to be enjoying themselves in the pond and in the palace on the pages of *The Frog Prince*.

In 1986 at the age of seventy-nine, Paul Galdone died of a heart attack. He lived a long and happy life doing what he loved best and he left us many beautiful books to read and remember him by.

A Selection of Books by
Paul Galdone

What's in Fox's Sack
The Steadfast Tin Soldier (*Anderson-Galdone*)
Hans in Luck
Henny Penny
King of the Cats
Obedient Jack
The Tailypo (*Joanna & Paul Galdone*)
Puss in Boots
The Gingerbread Boy
The Horse, The Fox and The Lion
The Magic Porridge Pot
The Monkey and the Crocodile
The Teeny-Tiny Woman
The Town Mouse and the County Mouse

The Turtle and the Monkey
Three Aesop Fox Fables
The Three Bears
The Three Little Pigs
The Three Billy Goats Gruff
The Frog Prince
The Anatole Mouse Series (*Titus-Galdone*)
Rumpelstiltskin
Hansel and Gretel
The Greedy Old Fat Man
Little Bo-Peep
Gertrude the Goose Who Forgot (*Joanna & Paul Galdone*)
The Queen Who Couldn't Bake Gingerbread (*Van Woerkom-Galdone*)

Reprinted with permission of McGraw-Hill Book Company.
Cover illustration from *The Frog Prince*, written and illustrated by Paul Galdone. Copyright ©1975. Published by McGraw-Hill.

Ezra Jack Keats

"Kyu, Kyu" in Japanese. "Knaar, knaar" in Swedish. "Knirk, knirk" in Danish. Around the world, these are the sounds of Peter walking through the snow in Ezra Jack Keats' award winning book, *The Snowy Day.*

Children all over the world love the characters and pictures created by this American author and illustrator. There is an Ezra Jack Keats roller skating rink for children in Tokyo, that was built after his book *Skates* helped to make skating popular there. The children's reading room of the Warrensville, Ohio Public Library is also named for him. He was the Guest of Honor at the openings of both of these places.

Ezra Jack Keats grew up in a large city, Brooklyn, New York. He lived in a third floor apartment in a neighborhood considered "tough." His parents were poor. Several of his books are about children who live in run-down sections of cities and do not have many toys or nice clothes. However, his books are not sad stories about poor children. Instead, they show us with great swirls of color the day-to-day events of people, work, animals, and games that are a part of a city child's life. If you look at *Apt.3, Pet Show, Goggles,* and *Whistle for Willie* you will see how the author's memories of his childhood in Brooklyn influenced his adult work as an artist and storyteller.

Mr. Keats started to paint when he was about four years old and the first thing he remembers painting on was a board. He covered it with blue and white paint to make a picture of fluffy clouds in a blue sky. One of his favorite places to paint was on a metal kitchen table in his apartment. He would cover it with pictures and his mother, who was proud of his talent, would call the neighbors to come in and look before it had to be wiped clean. His father did not want his son to become an artist because he thought it would be too hard for Ezra to earn a living. Although his father felt this way, he would, on occasion, bring his son home a tube of paint or take him to a museum to look at the great paintings.

Ezra Jack Keats taught himself to paint and did not have any formal training.

Completing high school he went right to work painting murals for a government project, drawing for Captain Marvel comic books, and then illustrating training manuals for the U.S. Army. Following his Army service he became an illustrator of stories for magazines, book jackets, and other people's books. After ten years of this he began to write and illustrate his own books, beginning with *The Snowy Day.*

Many years before he had ever thought of doing children's books, he was looking through a magazine and discovered four photographs of a little boy about four years old. The photographs of the little boy's face, actions, and personality seemd to touch his heart. He cut out the photos and stuck them on his studio wall. Twenty-two years later these photographs became the little boy named Peter in *The Snowy Day.* During the creation of this book Ezra Jack Keats began experimenting with a technique called collage, where he used bits of patterned paper to supplement the painting. This was a new art style for Keats and one that he was surprised to find changed his way of working. He continued to use collage and the character, Peter, in many books that followed. Readers can watch Peter grow older in *Peter's Chair, Goggles, A Letter to Amy,* and *Pet Show.*

Ezra Jack Keats once said, *"Although I have no children of my own, my books have — in a special way — made me a parent. Peter and his friends grow, have fun, problems, fears, and successes — and I've been with them through it all. I love these children, and it's been one of the greatest pleasures in my life to raise them and see them off into the world. While I'm working, I put all the illustrations up on my studio wall in page sequence. Often, I think I hear my characters talking to each other, whispering, making plans. The experiences in my books are those which all people share. Best of all, are the letters and the pictures of themselves that children send to me. I can now look up at my studio walls and see my friends — children of every color."*

After illustrating thirty-three books, twenty-two of which he also wrote, winning many awards and making many friends throughout the world, Ezra Jack Keats died of a heart attack in New York, in 1983. He was 67 years old.

A Selection of Books by
Ezra Jack Keats

A Letter to Amy
Apartment 3
Clementina's Cactus
Dreams
Goggles!
Hi, Cat!
Jennie's Hat
Kitten for a Day
Louie
Louie's Search
Maggie and the Pirate

Over in the Meadow
Peter's Chair
Pet Show
Psst! Doggie
Regards to the Man in the Moon
Skates!
The Snowy Day
The Trip
Whistle for Willie
Little Drummer Boy
John Henry: An American Legend

Aaagh!

Reprinted with permission.
Illustration from *Skates!* Written by Ezra Jack Keats.
Copyright ©1973. Published by Watts.

Steven Kellogg

Almost thirty years ago Steven Kellogg began telling stories to his sisters, Patti and Martha. The three children would sit on the floor and, for as long as they would listen, Steven would scribble drawings on big sheets of paper and make up stories to go with them. They would pass the papers around as Steven added more and more to the story. Today, Steven Kellogg is still doing pretty much the same thing. Only now he shares his stories with millions of readers, both young and old.

Steven Kellogg was born on October 26, 1941 in Norwalk, Connecticut, the son of Robert E. and Wilma Marie (Johnson) Kellogg. His favorite books as a child were those written and illustrated by Beatrix Potter and N.C. Wyeth. His special favorites were animal books.

His love of drawing and story telling continued from pre-school years, through elementary school, high school, and college. His artwork in college won him a year of study in Italy. When he returned to the United States he taught etching, painting, and printmaking at American University.

In 1967 he married Helen Hill. Most of his books are dedicated to their six children: Pam, Melanie, Laurie, Kim, Kevin and Colin. The family shares its big, old farmhouse in Sandy Hook, Connecticut with lots of pets. One of their lovable Great Danes, Pinkerton, inspired *Pinkerton, Behave!* and *Tallyho, Pinkerton!* Their oldest cat, Second Hand Rose, is the mixed-up little rascal of *A Rose for Pinkerton.* The pages of his books are filled with cuddly creatures.

While his stepchildren and pets have given him ideas for many of his books, he has written seventy-five books in almost twenty years. He also uses his own childhood memories and feelings.

If you have a big brother or sister who always makes you feel like you can't do anything right, you will really cheer for Henry in *Much Bigger Than Martin.* Or if you have ever felt as though all your friends have deserted you and left you on your own, you will know just how Kim feels in *Won't SOMEBODY Play With Me? Ralph's Secret Weapon* is a story of how a young boy, who has to do everything that grown-ups tell him to do, saves everybody from a giant sea serpent and finally gets to do what he wants to do. *The Orchard Cat* finds out that the only way to make a friend is to be a friend.

Mr. Kellogg loves to make picture books. *"Picture books introduce children to the world of art,"* he explains. His drawings are warm and sunny and match his words so well. By blending the right words with the right illustrations, he tries to create a *"feast for the eye and the ear."* You will find that his books are simply delicious!

Mr. Kellogg also believes that putting together a picture book is something like a director putting together a play. When the reader turns a page, it's like changing the scenery on a stage. So his books are full of surprises, some wacky, some scary, some hilarious.

Like the snowman in *The Mystery of the Missing Red Mitten,* Steven Kellogg's heart shows through in all of his stories. His readers hope that he will be "telling stories on paper" and passing them around for at least another twenty years and another seventy-five books.

A Selection of Books by
Steven Kellogg

A, My Name is Alice
Can I Keep Him?
The Island of the Skog
Much Bigger Than Martin
The Mysterious Tadpole
The Mystery of the Flying Orange Pumpkin
The Mystery of the Magic Green Ball
The Mystery of the Missing Red Mitten
Prehistoric Pinkerton

The Mystery of the Stolen Blue Paint
The Orchard Cat
Pinkerton Behave!
A Rose for Pinkerton
Tallyho, Pinkerton!
Won't SOMEBODY Play With Me?
Ralph's Secret Weapon
Chicken Little
Paul Bunyan

Reprinted with permission of Steven Kellogg.
Steven Kellogg (Dial Books Brochure) "S.K. Talks About Himself."
Illustration of Jimmy's Boa eating the wash.

Arnold Lobel

Arnold Lobel was born in Los Angeles, California on May 22, 1933. He died of a heart attack in Doctors Hospital in New York City on December 4, 1987. From the day he was born till the day he died he brought joy into people's hearts.

When he was a child, Arnold was not big and strong like some of the other youngsters and sometimes they teased him. To protect himself from these bullies and to amuse his classmates at school, he made up stories. This gave him good practice for his career as an author-illustrator.

In 1955 Arnold graduated as an artist from The Pratt Institute in Brooklyn, New York. That same year he married Anita Kempler who had also gone to Pratt and was also an artist. They were a perfect match! As the years passed, they both became famous authors of children's books. They even worked together on several books.

Arnold called himself a daydreamer. His mind always imagined the pictures before he thought of the words. In his 26 year career he created almost 100 books. He wrote and illustrated many of them himself. He also wrote stories that other artists illustrated. And he illustrated stories that other authors wrote.

In 1961 he illustrated his first book. It was titled *Red Tag Comes Back* and was written by Fred Phleger. It told the story of a salmon who swims upstream to lay eggs. This got him off to a good start because the very next year he illustrated his own story titled *A Zoo for Mister Muster.*

At that time he was living in a Brooklyn apartment with his wife and their two young children, Adrianna and Adam. The Prospect Park Zoo was right across the meadow from their apartment, and Arnold and the children often visited it while enjoying ice cream cones together. These trips to the zoo are what gave him the idea for the Mister Muster book. He dedicated it to Anita, Adrianna, and Adam.

As a child, Arnold had always loved listening to Mother Goose rhymes. He loved them all, even though many of them frightened him. As a grown-up illustrator, he was asked to publish a collection of his favorite Mother Goose rhymes. He included over 300 rhymes and created an illustration for each one. Many of his childhood memories helped him "daydream" his way through this project which took three years to complete.

When he was a little boy, he had always feared for the Three Blind Mice, so in his version, the mice are not blind. They wear sunglasses and are much faster runners than the Farmer's Wife. He said, *"As a child I liked mice, they were the only pets that my parents allowed me to have. In the book she doesn't get their tails."* Many of the other rhymes, though, he leaves just as scary as can be.

Some of Mr. Lobel's most popular books feature those two brown and green pop-eyed best buddies, *Frog and Toad.* They share walks together and yummy ice cream cones. They swim together and plan surprises for each other. They're best friends. Always together. Now and forever!

Mr. Lobel never looked back to the past. When he was asked which of his books was his favorite one, he answered that his favorite book was the next one. The one he hadn't done yet.

Arnold Lobel surely loved his work. The many honors and awards he received for his books must have made him proud. But he created them because he loved them. And as the moral of the story *"The Ostrich In Love"* says in his book *Fables:* *"Love can be its own reward."*

That is Mr. Lobel's reward.

A Selection of Books by
Arnold Lobel

A Zoo for Mister Muster
Prince Bertram the Bad
A Holiday for Mister Muster
Lucille
Giant John
The Bears in the Air
Martha, the Movie Mouse
The Great Blueness and Other Predicaments
Small Pig
Frog and Toad Are Friends
Ice-Cream Cone Coot and Other Rare Birds
On the Day Peter Stuyvesant Sailed into Town
Frog and Toad Together
Mouse Tales
The Man Who Took the Indoors Out
Owl at Home
Mouse Soup
Grasshopper on the Road
Days with Frog and Toad
A Treeful of Pigs
Fables
Whiskers and Rhymes
The Book of Pigericks: Pig Limericks

Gerald McDermott

Author, Illustrator, Film Maker he —
All these things Gerald McDermott can be

Gerald McDermott was born and raised in Detroit, Michigan. When he was four years old his parents recognized that he had a special talent and interest in art. His parents enrolled him in Saturday art classes at a local museum. He loved those classes and spent many happy hours at the museum learning to paint and draw.

When he was a teen-ager he became interested in film making. He was already attending a special high school of art and design in Detroit, but his school did not offer any classes in film. That didn't stop Gerald! He found an after-school job working for a television animation studio where he designed backgrounds for animated (cartoon-like) films. He began to make films with his friends, and in 1959 he won a national scholarship to a famous art and design school in New York City, called The Pratt Institute. Unfortunately, this school did not offer any film courses either. Gerald McDermott wanted to make films so much that he took a year off from school to work as a designer for a New York public television station, Channel 13. Pratt Institute was so impressed with his television experience and skill that they gave him permission to work by himself for college credit instead of attending their regular classes. He then set out to make his first professional animated film, *The Stonecutter,* a Japanese folktale.

In order to make animated films, many "still" drawings are photographed on movie film in a special way so that they appear to be moving when projected onto a screen by a movie projector. Six thousand "still" drawings were created for *The Stonecutter,* a short, six minute film. Each drawing had to be synchronized or matched perfectly to a note of background music. A film maker has to have a great deal of PATIENCE! Imagine drawing hundreds of pictures of the same subject making only tiny changes in each one!

Gerald McDermott created several more films after *The Stonecutter* and was then offered a chance to adapt his films into children's books. Usually the book is written before a film version is made, but with Mr. McDermott, the films came first and then the books. He had to learn to adapt and transfer his drawings and the story from film to paper. He was so successful in doing this that the book version of his film *Anansi the Spider* was named a Caldecott Honor Book for outstanding illustration and design in 1972. In 1975, Gerald McDermott won the Caldecott Medal with his book version of the film, *Arrow to the Sun.* Five of his films have also won international awards for their excellence.

Gerald McDermott is mainly interested in creating stories and films based on mythology and folktales of other cultures. He likes to work with stories where there is someone struggling to attain a goal or victory. In *Arrow to the Sun* a Pueblo Indian boy searches for his father. *In Daughter of Earth*, a Roman mother searches for her kidnapped daughter and in *The Stonecutter*, a Japanese man is searching for wealth. The pages of all his books are entirely filled with bright colors and shapes that contain symbols of the stories. Many of his characters have faces that are not handsome or beautiful, and some of his paintings can be scary, so don't read his books when you are alone on a dark, dark night!

Gerald McDermott has lived in Michigan, New York, and France. He presently lives in New Milford, Connecticut. He is famous all over the world for his films and books. Ask your teacher or librarian to show them to you. Perhaps you'll be able to have a Gerald McDermott film/book festival at your school.

A Selection of Books By
Gerald McDermott

Anansi the Spider: A Tale from the Ashanti
The Magic Tree: A Tale from the Congo
Arrow to the Sun: A Pueblo Indian Tale
The Stonecutter: A Japanese Folk Tale
The Voyage of Osiris: A Myth of Ancient Egypt
The Knight of the Lion
Papagayo the Mischief Maker
Sun Flight
Daughter of Earth: A Roman Tale
Daniel O'Rourke: An Irish Tale
The Musicians of the Sun: A Myth of Ancient Mexico

Peggy Parish

A dozen large rivers flow through South Carolina and empty into the Atlantic Ocean. One of these is called the Black River. Not too far from it is the little town of Manning where Margaret Cecile Parish was born and raised. She says that Manning was "a small town where everybody knew everybody. Life centered around the churches and schools."

"Peggy" remembers that she had been a sickly child when she was growing up and that everybody read to her all the time. She just loved hearing stories. All kinds of stories!

When Peggy grew up, she graduated from the Unviersity of South Carolina and became a school teacher. She taught in the "panhandle" part of the state of Oklahoma, and in the coal-mining areas of Kentucky. She eventually moved to New York where her first job was with the Girl Scouts. Next she was able to get a job teaching third grade in the Dalton School.

When South Carolina was first being settled in the 1700's, many people lived in log cabins and traded with the Indian people. This historical information about South Carolina was influential in many of Miss Parish's stories. When you read Miss Parish's books, you will discover that she has written many stories about the Indian people. In fact, she says that she got the idea for her first book, *Let's Be Indians* when her third grade class was studying all about them in social studies. Her funny *"Granny"* books also have Indians in them.

Miss Parish's most famous character is, of course, Amelia Bedelia. Amelia is that lovable housemaid who always manages to get things done in the strangest ways. She does what Mr. and Mrs. Rogers say, but she doesn't exactly do what they mean. For example, if you were to "dress a chicken" you would get it ready to be cooked. Not Amelia Bedelia! She dresses the chicken in pants and socks. In another story, she uses real sponges to make sponge cake. That makes it a little too chewy to eat!

Besides the Amelia Bedelia books, Peggy Parish has also written some very fine craft books and mystery books. If you like solving puzzles and codes, you will enjoy the adventures of Liza, Jed, and Bill in the *Haunted House, Clues in the Woods,* and *Key to the Treasure.* The three children come upon many mysterious things such as ghosts and secret messages, but they always stick together. After all, that's what friends are for.

When asked about her early schooling, Miss Parish says that she honestly has only pleasant school memories. Today she is living back in her old hometown of Manning, South Carolina, where she has seen many of the teachers she had in grammar school. She even dedicated *Teach Us, Amelia Bedelia* to *"Miss Rose, my first-grade teacher, who introduced me to the magic of words, with love."* She has also enjoyed seeing her favorite high school English teacher. She says, *"They are all still lovely people."* They must be very proud of their famous star pupil.

Peggy loves to work in her garden and, while she is weeding it, she thinks of stories. When the sun gets too hot to work, she goes inside and writes down the ideas she had while she was gardening. It's as if the seeds of her ideas get planted in the garden and they blossom a little while later when she writes them down on paper in the house.

Miss Parish has a large family of cats who help her with her gardening. She plants the seeds and the cats dig them up! You can learn more about cats in her book titled, *The Cats' Burglar.*

If you think Peggy Parish loves her work you are right! When asked if she has a favorite among all the books she has written, she says *"No, each one is my child."* Just as a parent loves each child in the family, Peggy Parish loves each one of her books.

We can be grateful to her for sharing all her "children" with us.

A Selection of Books by
Peggy Parish

My Golden Book of Manners
Good Hunting Little Indian
Let's Be Indians
Willy Is My Brother
Amelia Bedelia
Thank You, Amelia Bedelia
The Story of Grains: Wheat, Corn, and Rice
Amelia Bedelia and the Surprise Shower
Key to the Rescue
Let's Be Early Settlers With Daniel Boone
Clues in the Woods
Little Indian
A Beastly Circus
Jumper Goes to School
Granny and the Indians

Ootah's Lucky Day
Granny and the Desperadoes
Costumes to Make
Snapping Turtle's All Wrong Day
Sheet Magic: Games, and Gifts from Old Sheets
Haunted House
Granny, the Baby, and the Big Gray Thing
Play Ball, Amelia Bedelia
Too Many Rabbits
Dinosaur Time
December Decorations: A Holiday How-To Book
Pirate Island Adventure
Good Work, Amelia Bedelia
Teach Us, Amelia Bedelia

Reprinted with permission
Illustration of Amelia Bedelia "Putting out the lights" as found in
Amelia Bedelia, Illustration by Fritz Siebel.
Copyright ©1963. Published by Harper & Row.

Bill Peet

William B. Peet was born in Grandview, Indiana on January 29, 1915. His father, Orion Hopkins, was a salesman who sold everything from house paint to popcorn machines. His mother, Emma, was a teacher. When Bill was three years old his family moved to Indianapolis where they lived about a block away from the railroad.

Bill has always been interested in the outdoors and at the age of about seven or eight he read everything he could find in the library about wildlife. His favorite book was *Wahb: The Biography of a Grizzly.*

Until he was about twelve, his family lived near the outskirts of town. On Saturdays, with his two brothers and friends from the neighborhood, Bill used to go on hikes out into "the open countryside with its small rivers and creeks that went winding through the rolling hills."

One of Bill Peet's favorite boyhood memories was visiting his grandfather's farm in southern Indiana. "It was the first train trip for me and my two brothers, something of a treat in itself." All along the way he gazed out the window at the scenery he loved most: barns, haystacks, farm animals, small towns, rivers, creeks, and forests. Grandfather's farm was much more interesting than the countryside around Indianapolis. It was much more rustic.

Bill's first visit to the zoo was during a trip to Cincinatti. He had saved his money from selling newspapers so that he could buy lots of film for his box camera. When he got to the zoo he took pictures of every animal, clicking away all afternoon. Later he found out that the shutter had not been working, and not one picture turned out! The next time he went to the zoo he played it safe, he took along a sketch pad and pencil. This time if a picture didn't turn out it would be his own fault.

Since his mother was a handwriting teacher and supervisor of penmanship in the Indianapolis schools for over thrity-five years, there was always plenty of paper around the house for drawing, which was Bill's main hobby. *"I drew just about anything that came to mind, all sorts of animals* (including dragons), *trains, fire engines, racing cars, airplanes, gladiators, pioneers, World War I battles, football games, prize fights, or what have you."*

Bill just couldn't get enough art when he was in grammar school. Even in his regular classes he would keep a pad in his desk and sketch pictures when his teacher wasn't looking. One day his teacher caught him. Turning to the class she said, "I want you to see what William has been doing!" With an amused smile on her face, the teacher turned the pages for all the children to see. Bill was surprised! His teacher was very proud of his work and encouraged Bill to do something with his art someday. That was his wish too. More than anything else in the world!

After high school Bill continued his art studies at the John Herron Art Institute in Indianapolis. For three years he studied drawing, painting, and design. He met his wife, Margaret while he was in art school. He decided to marry her as soon as he could earn some money as an artist. He moved to California when he heard there were lots of jobs for artists making films there. Now he could marry Margaret. He worked for Walt Disney for 27 years. He was a writer and illustrator for many wonderful films, including *101 Dalmatians*.

While their two sons were growing up, Bill would make up bedtime stories for them each night. Soon he decided that it was time for him to work on his own, so he began writing stories for children. His first book was *Hubert's Hair-Raising Adventure*. And every book since then has been just as welcome as the first! Eleanor the Elephant, Eli the Lion, Chester the Pig, Pamela Camel, Cyrus the Sea Serpent, Buford the Bighorn Sheep, Droofus the Dragon — these are just some of the delightful characters that fill the more than thirty books Bill Peet has written and illustrated.

Bill Peet's favorite foods are spaghetti and fried chicken. His favorite place is the forest. And his favorite memory is still his grandfather's farm. If Bill could have three wishes they would be for: Peace on Earth, that no one would go hungry, and that people of all colors would live together as friends.

**It's easy to see that Bill Peet is one
"ding-dong-doozie" of a guy!**

A Selection of Books by
Bill Peet

The Ant and the Elephant
Big Bad Bruce
Buford, The Little Bighorn
The Caboose Who Got Loose
Capyboppy
Chester the Worldly Pig
Cowardly Clyde
Cyrus The Unsinkable Sea Serpent
Eli
Ella
Encore for Eleanor
Farewell to Shady Glade
Fly Homer Fly
The Gnats of Knotty Pine
How Droofus The Dragon Lost His Head

Hubert's Hair-Raising Adventure
Huge Harold
Jennifer and Josephine
Kermit the Hermit
The Luckiest One of All
Merle the High Flying Squirrel
No Such Things
Smokey
The Spooky Tail of Prewitt Peacock
The Whingdingdilly
The Wump World
Count Down to Christmas
Pamela Camel
Kweek

Reprinted with permission of Bill Peet.
Sketch of *Whingdingdilly* as found in autobiographical brochure,
"Bill Peet" (no copyright)

Margret and H.A. Rey

Curious George, Pretzel, and Katy No-Pocket are famous animals created by this husband and wife writing team. Margret usually writes the stories and H.A., which stands for "Hans Augusto," does the illustrations. They help each other when creating a book and enjoy working together even though they sometimes argue about the story or the pictures. Margret says that their work is just about the only thing they ever fight about. The Reys have written books together, and separately, and with other people.

Margret and Hans were both born in Germany and went to school there. After they were married they lived in Europe and South America before moving to New York in 1940. *Curious George* was their first book in the United States. In 1946 they became American citizens.

Writing is hard work for them and often a book will take as long as a year to finish. Ideas for their books come at anytime and anywhere. Sometimes even while taking a bath.

H.A. Rey lived close to a zoo when he was a child in Germany and that is where he learned to love animals. He could imitate animal sounds and could roar so well that he sounded like a lion. Once, years later, when making a personal appearance in the Atlanta, Georgia Civic Auditorium, he roared for 3,000 children, much to their delight.

The Reys have always had pets. There have been unusual ones like monkeys and alligators, but they have also had dogs, newts, chameleons, and turtles. You will find that most of their books are about animals. However, H.A. also wrote two books on astronomy that can be found in most libraries.

Their *Curious George* books are famous all over the world and have been translated into a dozen different languages. If you were in Japan you could buy *Curious George* printed in Japanese!

The Reys lived in New York for many years. In 1963 they moved to Cambridge, Massachusetts. On August 26, 1977, Hans Augusto Rey died after a long illness. He was 79 years old. Margret is still living and working on new books.

A Selection of Books by Margret and H.A. Rey

Curious George
Curious George Takes a Job
Curious George Rides a Bike
Curious George Flies a Kite
Curious George Learns the Alphabet
Curious George Goes to the Hospital
Cecily G. and the Nine Monkeys
Katy No-Pocket
Where's My Baby?

Anybody At Home?
Feed the Animals
See the Circus
The Stars - A New Way to See Them
Find the Constellations
Elizabite
Pretzel
Spotty
Billy's Picture

Maurice Sendak

Maurice Sendak, creator of *Where The Wild Things Are,* knew he wanted to be a writer and illustrator before he ever went to school. His childhood was spent in Brooklyn, New York where he was the youngest of three children. His father made up wonderful stories to tell the family. Sendak's happiest memories of those days were drawing, reading, and listening to stories with his brother and father. He says that he had a very nice childhood, but wasn't a particularly happy child. Many of the famous jagged tooth monsters from his *"Wild Things"* book are modeled on the uncles and aunts who used to come to Sunday dinner in Brooklyn. Maurice Sendak remembers them as being very *"big people who might eat him up."*

When he was old enough he found an after school job working for All American Comics drawing in backgrounds for their *Mutt and Jeff* comic strips. His experience working with comics later influenced his book, *In The Night Kitchen.* Having been a Mickey Mouse fan since childhood, he even has a comic book related hobby. He has a large collection of Mickey Mouse toys, lamps, coin banks, pictures, clocks, statues, and other objects.

Where The Wild Things Are is his most famous book, winning the Caldecott Medal in 1963 and continuing to be a best selling children's book for the last twenty-five years. It has sold nearly two million copies in English and has been translated into sixteen languages. There are Max and 'Wild Things' dolls, posters, a movie, and even an opera. Seven years ago Oliver Knussen wrote the music for a "Wild Things" opera and Maurice Sendak wrote the words and designed the sets and costumes. He has also done set designs and costumes for a movie version of *The Nutcracker* and for an animated television special called *Really Rosie* starring the Nutshell Kids. *Really Rosie* was later performed as a musical on the Broadway stage with children playing the parts of the Nutshell Kids.

Besides drawing and designing for the stage and film, Maurice Sendak has worked with many other authors. Ruth Krauss *(A Hole is To Dig)*, Else Minarik *(the Little Bear books)*, and Meindert DeJong *(Wheel on the School)* are some of the well known writers whose books he has illustrated. He also has written and illustrated many books by himself. His books come in all sizes. Some are small enough to fit in one hand like *The Nutshell Library*. Others like *The Nutcracker* are much larger. He is currently working on a newly discovered Grimm fairy tale called *Dear Millie* to be published in the United States for the first time. Sendak has been interested in the Grimm fairy tales for many years. He has illustrated a two volume set of Grimm tales called *The Juniper Tree*.

The children and animals in Maurice Sendak's books express their feelings very openly. Max misbehaves and is sent to bed, Pierre "doesn't care," and Rosie says, "she's a great big deal!" Sendak says he doesn't set out to write books for children, but books for himself. It just so happens that children like them too. *"Children know what's real and what's not real,"* he claims.

Maurice Sendak, who has never married, lives in Connecticut with two pet dogs. There is a woods near his home and everyday he interrupts his work long enough to take long walks with the dogs. *Higglety Pigglety Pop!* is the story of his pet Sealyham terrier, Jennie, who goes out into the world to look for something more than she already has. The 'real' Jennie lived with him for many years before she died of old age. He wrote *Higglety Pigglety Pop!* so she would be known and remembered forever.

Mr. Sendak works in a large studio in his home. There are Mickey Mouse objects all around his studio work area. He likes to listen to classical music when he works and Mozart is his favorite composer. Sometimes pictures of Mozart will appear in surprising places on the pages of his books or in his set designs. You have to have sharp eyes to notice them, but look in *Outside Over There* and see if you can find one.

Maurice Sendak is very serious about his work. His office is his studio and he works there almost everyday. Each project is done with a great deal of thought and attention to detail. Maurice Sendak agrees with his character, Pierre, who at the end of the book shouts, ***"Yes, indeed I care!"***

A Selection of Books by
Maurice Sendak

King Grisly-Beard
Charlotte and the White Horse
A Hole is to Dig
Open House for Butterflies
The Art of Maurice Sendak
Little Bear Books
The Juniper Tree and Other Tales by Grimm
Alligators All Around
Chicken Soup with Rice
Higglety Pigglety Pop!
Nutshell Library
Outside Over There
Pierre
Really Rosie
Seven Little Monsters
Where the Wild Things Are

Dr. Seuss

Have you ever seen a Tufted Mazzurka from the Island of Yerka? Or Brown Barba-loots who eat Truffula Fruits? You probably haven't, unless you are a fan of Dr. Seuss.

Dr. Seuss, whose real name is Theodor Seuss Geisel (pronounced GUY-zel), was born in 1904 in Springfield, Massachusetts. His father, Theodor, was in charge of the Springfield public parks. His mother's last name had been Seuss before she married Mr. Geisel and that's where Dr. Seuss got his name.

Theodor loved to draw as a young child and this interest grew as he got older. But when he was in high school, a teacher told him to give it up, "You will never learn to draw." Luckily, Theodor did not give up drawing.

When Dr. Seuss tries to draw a horse, or a zebra, he really tries to draw one in the very best way he can. But what he draws does not always look like the real thing. The same thing happens with the words for his stories. If he can't think of just the right word to use, he makes one up! And that is what makes Dr. Seuss so special!

After high school, he thought he might like to become a teacher, but this did not work out. While serving in the Army during World War II he worked as an artist and created two award-winning films. Later, in 1951, he wrote a children's cartoon called *Gerald McBoing-Boing.* This film also won an Academy Award and is still thought to be one of the best children's movies ever made.

Before the war, he had spent twelve years drawing cartoons to sell insect spray for a large oil company. During this time he drew thousands of funny cartoons for the company, but to keep himself amused he began writing stories for children. It was for these stories, that he first used the name Dr. Seuss.

His first book was *And To Think I Saw It On Mulberry Street.* This book had been turned down by 28 publishers before it was finally published in 1937.

To get ideas for new books he sometimes just doodles some silly drawings for characters. Then he puts these different characters together to see what might happen. The rest of the story seems to come along all by itself.

One of his most famous books, *Horton Hatches the Egg* came about quite by accident. Sitting on his desk was a drawing of an elephant that he had been working on. A breeze from a nearby open window blew the drawing onto a sketch of a tree and BINGO! The story of lovable "Horton" was hatched.

Dr. Seuss, or Theo Le Seig, as he is also known, is a hard worker. He may have to write a story over and over many times before he gets it just the way he wants it. He might fill a thousand sheets of paper with new ideas, changing them around as he goes. And the finished book will be only about 64 pages long. A book like *The Cat in the Hat* could take over a year to complete.

It took Dr. Seuss twelve months of thinking about the real meaning of Christmas before he was ready to write a story about it. Then, in one week he wrote *How the Grinch Stole Christmas.*

Dr. Seuss and his wife live on top of a high mountain in La Jolla, California. Since he is very interested in rocks, it is not surprising that there is a beautiful rock garden in their yard.

The "Lorax," the "Cat in the Hat," and many other Dr. Seuss characters are known and loved by children all over the world. His books have been published in Japan, Israel, Germany, Italy, Brazil, Great Britain, Norway, Sweden, Denmark, and Holland.

When you read his books you can be sure of one thing:

"From there to here,
from here to there,
funny things are everywhere."

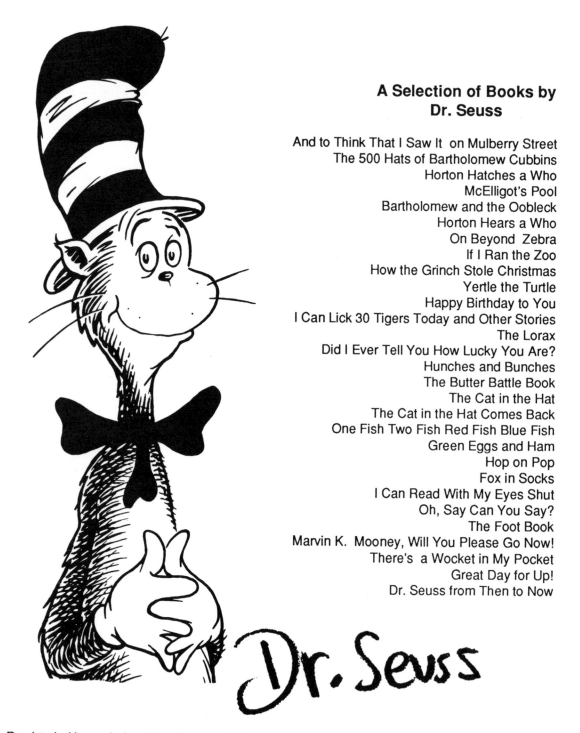

A Selection of Books by Dr. Seuss

And to Think That I Saw It on Mulberry Street
The 500 Hats of Bartholomew Cubbins
Horton Hatches a Who
McElligot's Pool
Bartholomew and the Oobleck
Horton Hears a Who
On Beyond Zebra
If I Ran the Zoo
How the Grinch Stole Christmas
Yertle the Turtle
Happy Birthday to You
I Can Lick 30 Tigers Today and Other Stories
The Lorax
Did I Ever Tell You How Lucky You Are?
Hunches and Bunches
The Butter Battle Book
The Cat in the Hat
The Cat in the Hat Comes Back
One Fish Two Fish Red Fish Blue Fish
Green Eggs and Ham
Hop on Pop
Fox in Socks
I Can Read With My Eyes Shut
Oh, Say Can You Say?
The Foot Book
Marvin K. Mooney, Will You Please Go Now!
There's a Wocket in My Pocket
Great Day for Up!
Dr. Seuss from Then to Now

Shel Silverstein

Shel Silverstein took fourteen years to write just one of the poems in his book *Where the Sidewalk Ends.* That is because he is only one inch tall! Or, so he says in the poem. (Do you think it could be true?)

Mr. Silverstein has been drawing cartoons and writing stories, songs, and poems for over thirty years. Children and adults of all ages enjoy his jokes, his dreams, his hopes and his joys. Mr. Silverstein does not talk about himself very much, so we don't know too much about his personal life. In fact, he says that if you want to know about him, just read his books. That is where you will find the real Shel Silverstein.

One of his most famous and well-loved books is *The Giving Tree.* If you have a favorite tree that you like to climb, or if you have a treehouse in your yard, you can imagine how the little boy in *The Giving Tree* feels when the tree gives him shade from the heat and fruit to eat. But the tree does not stop there. The book tells all about the special friendship that grows between the Boy and the Tree. *Where The Sidewalk Ends* is an enchanted place. You have probably been to this place in your own imagination. It is a place where you can fly in a shoe; you can write inside a lion; you can play music with your belly or your nose. It's a place where you can even put a "For Sale" sign on your pesty brother or sister!

Mr. Silverstein enjoys his work and thinks that everyone should live their lives doing what they like to do best, no matter what other people think. You should find out what you enjoy and what you are good at, and keep at it. Whenever you get discouraged or feel like you just can't do anything right, just remember this bit of Shel Silverstein advice:

> *"Then listen close to me —*
> *Anything can happen, child,*
> *ANYTHING can be."*

A Selection of Books by Shel Silverstein

Lafcadio, The Lion Who Shot Back
A Giraffe and a Half
The Missing Piece

The Missing Piece Meets the Big O
A Light in the Attic
The Giving Tree

Brian Wildsmith

Brian Wildsmith was born in a small mining village in Yorkshire, England in 1930. When he was ten he won a scholarship to study chemistry at De La Salle College and he went there intending to become a chemist. However, six years later he tried painting and he decided that being an artist was what he wanted to do with his life. He left his chemistry studies and enrolled in a school of art. He studied painting and drawing until he was old enough to be asked to serve in the English Army. When he was discharged from the Army, he became an art teacher. After three years of teaching art he decided to spend all his time working as a free-lance artist illustrating books and book jackets. Most of his first books were illustrated with line drawings that were not in color except for the covers. Later on he was able to get full color book assignments from editors in England and America. His first books using full color illustrations throughout were *Tales from the Arabian Nights* published in 1961 and *Brian Wildsmith's ABC* published in 1962. The ABC book won the Kate Greenaway Award for distinguished illustration that year.

His book illustrations are done using a method of painting called gouache (*Pronounced "gwash"*) mixed with impasto. Gouache is when an artist mixes water colors with a preparation of gum, made from a plant. Impasto means an application of thick layers of paint. Brian Wildsmith mixes his colors with water and gum and then puts them on paper in thick layers to achieve the special Wildsmith effect. If you look at his picture book illustrations you will notice how bright the colors are and how the pages are filled with many details of design. He says that where he lived when he was growing up in England, *"Everything was gray. There wasn't any color. It was up to my imagination and I had to draw in my head."* In his picture books every page is full of color because as an artist he believes that children respond to colors, shapes and forms. He has often said that children understand the feeling of beauty before they understand how it is created.

Brian Wildsmith has created more than thirty picture books. Some of his latest ones are designed with split pages where the center or 'split' page serves as a perfect part of the completed picture on either side of it. *Pelican* and *Daisy* are split page books that resemble pieces of a giant puzzle that fit together perfectly to create a beautiful whole as the reader turns each page.

Mr. Wildsmith not only illustrates books but he also writes many of his own stories. He likes to write his own versions of fables and Bible stories, as well as books about animals and birds. He has illustrated a book of poetry and soon will publish *Brian Wildsmith's Book of Favorite Bedtime Tales.* His books have been published in seven different countries and have won many awards. In 1965 he designed a set of Christmas cards for the United Nations (UNESCO) and they sold nearly seven million copies around the world. He has also designed a set of posters depicting the months of the year and they can be found in art and book stores and on the walls of libraries and classrooms.

Brian Wildsmith and his wife, Aurelie, have four grown children. The Wildsmiths have homes in two different countries. They spend part of the year in southern France and the rest of the time in London, England where they live in a flat (apartment).

When people tell him that his pictures are too beautiful to be in books for children and should be hanging in art galleries and museums, Brian Wildsmith says, *"Nothing we give to children can be too beautiful for them to have."* He has given us many beautiful books and we give him our thanks and appreciation in return.

A Selection of Books by
Brian Wildsmith

1 2 3
Animal Games
Animal Homes
Animal Shapes
Animal Tracks
Bible Stories
Birds
Circus
Fishes
The Hare and the Tortoise
The Hunter and His Dog
The Lazy Bear

The Lion and the Rat
The Little Wood Duck
The Miller, the Boy and the Donkey
Mother Goose
The North Wind and the Sun
The Owl and the Woodpecker
Professor Noah's Spaceship
The Rich Man and the Shoemaker
Seasons
Squirrels
The True Cross

What the Moon Saw
Wild Animals
The Twelve Days of Christmas
Daisy
Pelican
Python's Party
Maurice Maeterlinck's Blue Bird
Brian Wildsmith's ABC Book
Give A Dog A Bone
The Bear's Adventure
Cat on a Mat
Apple Bird

Reprinted with permission of Oxford University Press.
Illustration of the sun from, *What The Moon Saw*, written by Brian Wildsmith. Oxford University Press.
Copyright © 1978.